Knot Tying Book for Everyday Occasion

A Knot Tying Guide on How to Tie 25 of the Most Important Rope Knots with Step By Step Knot Tying Instructions

By

Garrick Boyd

Copyright © 2021 – Garrick Boyd

All rights reserved

No part of this publication may be reproduced, distributed, or transmitted in any form or by any means, including photocopying, recording, or other electronic or mechanical methods, without the prior written permission of the publisher, except in the case of brief quotations embodied in reviews and certain other non-commercial uses permitted by copyright law.

Disclaimer

This publication is designed to provide competent and reliable information regarding the subject matter covered. However, the views expressed in this publication are those of the author alone, and should not be taken as expert instruction or professional advice. The reader is responsible for his or her own actions.

The author hereby disclaims any responsibility or liability whatsoever that is incurred from the use or application of the contents of this publication by the purchaser or reader. The purchaser or reader is hereby responsible for his or her own actions.

Table of Contents

Introduction 7

Chapter 1 9

Essentials of Knot Tying 9

    What is Knot Tying? 9

    History of Knot Tying 9

    Application Areas of Knot Tying 10

Chapter 2 13

Knot Tying Terminologies 13

Chapter 3 18

Getting Started with Knot Tying 18

    Rope Material 18

        Natural Rope Materials 19
        Synthetic Rope Materials 22
    Rope Construction 27

    Choosing the Right Rope 31

    Choosing the Right Knot 42

Tips and Techniques of Tying a Rope Knot 47

How to Untie Rope Knots 65

Caring for Your Rope Knots 69

Chapter 4 73

Everyday Knot Tying Projects 73

Barrel Sling 73

Plank Sling 75

Jury Mast Knot 77

Three-Way Sheet Bend 80

Poldo Tackle 82

Chain Stitch Lashing 84

Half Hitching 88

Marline Hitching 91

Diamond Hitch 93

Trucker's Hitch 97

Ocean Plait 101

Hiking Knot 106

Square Knot 108

Two-Half Hitches 108

Sailor's Knot 110

Fishing Knot 111

Bowline Knot 112

Eight-Strand Square Plait 113

Three-Strand Braid 114

Two-Strand Braid Knot 116

Braid Knot 118

Endless Double Chain 120

Endless Simple Chain 122

Clove Hitch 123

Taut Line Hitch 124

Chapter 5 126

Resolving Knot Tying Common Mistakes 126

Chapter 6 130

Knot Tying Frequently Asked Questions 130

Conclusion 133

Introduction

Knot tying is an art that involves the creation of decorative materials with the use of thread, ropes, and strings. Knots are of different kinds and each has a particular purpose it works to achieve. Some of these things include finishing knots, macramé, climbing knots, sailing knots, etc. There are also hitches, bends, loop knots, splices, and several other techniques tied to knotting that can create something beautiful. These designs are usually made with natural strings of rope or synthetic ones. The kind of rope used largely determines how the knot will look like and its quality too. Funny enough, to make these designs, you do not need a machine or the big tools other works of art require. For all your projects, you will need a well of confidence and creativity. In fact, creativity is one of the biggest things you should have. That is why this book, **Knot Tying Book for Everyday Occasion,** will help you to deal with the first stage of getting creative.

After trying out the several projects penned here, you can be sure that you'd easily get to overcome that stage. Apart from what has been emphasized in the above paragraph, you will see many secret tips that will leave your knots looking like one of the best in the world. There are also safety procedures and techniques that will guide you in tying ropes efficiently. Several images are incorporated into this book that will help you understand the techniques of tying knots.

Chapter 1

Essentials of Knot Tying

What is Knot Tying?

Knot-tying is an art that involves braiding ropes in ornate designs and structures. Ropes are made by closely intertwined fibers and yarns, which together, would create something compact with greater tensile strength than each component material. Knot-tying serves several purposes apart from those tied to decoration. They could be used as hitches, bends, loop knots, splices, and so on. So, linking threads together will create knots. This step is produced by linking the end of one thread line called the working end through a circular loop. Then, you draw it tight to get the knot style mentioned earlier.

History of Knot Tying

Knots won't exist if ropes didn't themselves. Unfortunately, since ropes are formed from degradable materials, they don't stand the test of time in most scenarios. However, it is no doubt that ropes have existed since the start of time. Before cars and trains came into existence, man depended heavily on ropes to drag boats and animals. This technique was especially favored by sailors and canoe men as the strong grip offered by the knotted ropes prevented the heavy water currents from driving the boats off.

The Bowline knot was a common knot that served this purpose well, and so, you'd find ropes with this kind of knot in the evacuated ships owned by the Egyptians. The Chinese kind of knotting is majorly for decorative purposes and it constitutes a major element of the Chinese folk art. There were several ropes listed in the historical timelines of China and they include the bottle sling, the bowline, Cat's paw, clove hitch, cow hitch, overhand bend, and overhand knot. According to the details offered by archeologists, human beings worked with knotted ropes to record a track of events, folklores, and dates. They were also used during prayers and religious confessions.

Application Areas of Knot Tying

Knot-tying is a very important technique that is useful in several areas of life and over the years, its functions have been modified to serve more purposes. So in this section, we will take a dive into the everyday uses of knot-tying.

- Knotted ropes, in primitive cultures, were used to keep track of dates, important events and to remember important folk tales.

- The knotted ropes are used as snares for animals and to catch fishes. Nets are also ropes, only that their bodies are linked with tinier pieces of strings and fibers.

- A bow knot will keep your shoelaces tied up.

- A slip knot will be suitable for ropes used for the purpose of hunting and camping.

- Stopper knots prevent an already splintered rope from fraying at the edges.

- Looped ropes work as attachment centers. You could easily slip hooks through the loops in case you need to get a firm grip on something far away.

- Hitches will secure ropes to objects. For example, you could secure your rafts to pillars.

- Knotted ropes, help with climbing and rescue missions.

- Ropes made from sisal satisfy all sorts of purposes.

- Ropes made from coir function as boat fenders, rope rigging, etc.

Basket crafters, bookbinders, cobblers, fireman, fishermen, peddlers, and farmers hold the rope knotting techniques in higher significance because of their everyday uses in their daily life affairs.

Chapter 2

Knot Tying Terminologies

Knot-tying is a wide art that has several terms that might seem strange to a beginner. Now, we'll quickly scan through a few to get you familiarized with them.

1. **Standing end**: When thinking of knots, imagine how you'd tie your shoelaces so tightly that they don't come loose again after. On studying ropes, you'd see that there's usually a portion that doesn't engage in the tying process. It just sits and acts as the base for the knots you make. This side of the string is called the running end.

2. **Working end**: We'd also use a shoelace as a point of reference for this term. The two ends of the string that you grip in your fingers and in turn, lace through the shoe's holes are called the working ends. The working ends have another name, which is called the running end. They are responsible for forming the knots you see.

3. **Bight**: This term is defined by the bent edges of a string or rope. If you curved a string into a U-shape, that curvy part is identified as the bight. Bights range

from a few inches long to even a few feet long. It all depends on the purpose it is serving.

4. **Loop**: Loops are formed from bights. We already established the fact that bights have U-shapes. So, when one curved edge of the 'U' meets the other side, a small circle is formed. This circle is called the loop. Loops are made in two different ways. The first one is the overhand loop. For this kind of loop, the running side is the one that crosses over the standing end. However, in the underhand loop, the standing end moves first and crosses over the running end. These loops serve the purpose of attachment of objects like carabineers.

5. **Crossing point**: This term is derived from a loop. When the two parts of the 'U' segment of the bight cross, they form the loop quite alright, but the point at which they meet is called the crossing point.

6. **Elbow**: An elbow constitutes two loops in close range. For example, when you have a very long rope, you could form two or more bights. When a knot is tied at the bottom of each bight, a loop is formed. When the two loops are brought together, you get an elbow.

7. **Bend**: A bend in knot-tying is a knot that joins the two lengths of rope together. Take note that each length of rope here is a separate unit.

8. **Hitch**: A hitch is a knot that you make when you need to attach strings to the span of an object. For example, you will need to make a hitch knot when you make a knot around a nail or rod.

9. **Friction hitch**: This kind of hitch, just as the name implies, helps to fight the effect of friction when carrying out activities like climbing. You know, when climbing up a hill, your palms could suddenly become sweaty. The extra knot on the rope will help ensure that you have an extra knot while climbing. The friction hitch is also referred to as the slide-and-grip knot. So, as you move, you slide the extra knot up. In friction hitches, the rope is tied on to another in a loose fashion.

10. **Whipping**: This term describes the knot that you make at the end of a string to prevent the previous knots from loosening.

11. **Stopper knots:** These are temporary kinds of whipping that you can eventually get rid of.

12. **Splice**: Here, two ropes are joined by twisting their strands out of the weave they were in before and then re-weaving them into one piece.

13. **Slipped knot:** This kind of knot is usually not permanent or fixed. It can move when one end constituting a tie is pulled, even to lengths where it gets loosened. So, to obtain loose knots, stick with using slipped knot technique.

14. **Noose**: A noose is a kind of loop joints that grows tighter as you pull at one of its edges.

15. **Seizing**: This term is related to the 'Elbow' term. It is a kind of knot that holds two ropes by their sides to form a loop.

16. **Lashing**: For this term, we'll consider the structure of a cross. There's usually a portion that runs horizontally and another that runs vertically. Instead of using nails to join them at their middles, you could use a rope. And that method of knotting is called lashing.

17. **Jamming**: Once you make some knots, it could get pretty difficult to untie them. That is what we refer to as 'jamming.'

18. **Fraps**: This term refers to loops that are made in directions perpendicular to the lashing wraps. This kind of loop helps to tighten rope joints.

19. **Flake**: Whenever you hear that a rope has been flaked, it also means that it has been coiled up.

20. **Dressing**: Just like how you'd dress a cake to make it more beautiful, you could get knots ordered in a way that will increase their joint strength, as well as decrease their susceptibility to jamming.

21. **Capsizing**: Sometimes, this term is made intentionally or unintentionally. A capsized tie possesses a ruined look, and it could be because of strings that were tied up wrongly. Capsized knots can also be an additional source of strength for most weak knots.

22. **Cordage**: A general name that describes the majority of ropes and cords. They are mostly used to describe ropes using for the rigging of a ship.

Chapter 3

Getting Started with Knot Tying

Rope Material

Ropes are made from several kinds of starting materials like Manila hemp, hemp, straw, sisal, jute, polypropylene, nylon, polyesters, and polyethylene. These examples are combinations of natural and synthetic materials.

Natural ropes are made out of several kinds of fiber and all of these contribute to the strength and durability of the rope. However, natural ropes don't have as much strength as synthetic ropes. Synthetic ropes have higher tensile strengths and greater resistance to rotting than natural ropes. Natural ropes are also easily destroyed by light, mildew, water, and mold but are resistant to heat. Synthetic ropes are only destroyed by ultraviolet light and can easily burn if exposed to fire. They are also susceptible to getting slippery.

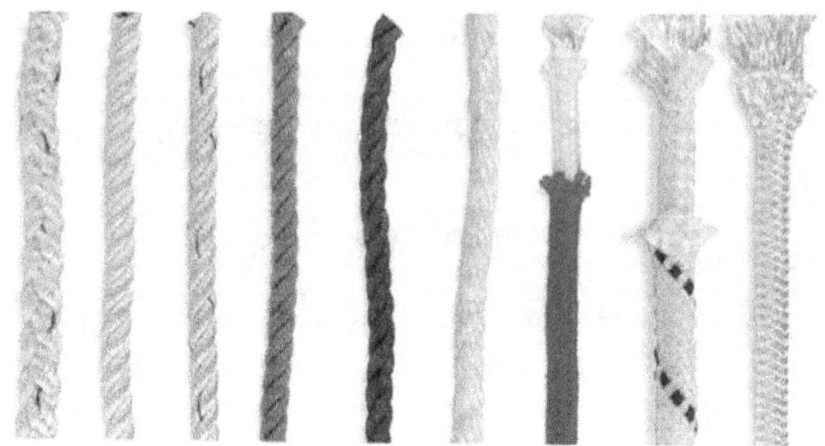

Natural Rope Materials

Natural ropes are mostly made from chopped and combed plant fibers obtained from stems, (flax, jute, etc.), leaves, (sisal, hemp), seeds, (cotton), and other parts like the fibrous shells of coconut; coir, hair from camels, date palms, grass, wool, silk, reeds, esparto, and so on. Once these materials are obtained, they are twisted into yarns and then rolled in anticlockwise directions to form strands. These ropes are made when these strands are rolled clock wisely. Below are examples of natural rope materials.

1. **Manila Hemp**

• Often referred to as manila hemp, manila is one of the strongest ropes used out there.

• It was the only option before synthetic rope materials were used.

• Its other name, hemp, does not mean that it was made from the hemp plant. Manila is obtained from the Abaca plant.

• It shrinks the moment water touches it. So, before any rope made from manila is used, it is first immersed in water to first contract to a size that can be used to make knots.

• When a manila rope is wet, do not make knots on it as it could lead to the issue of jamming, i.e., difficulty in loosening knots. Instead, wait for it to dry before knotting it.

• Even though it is mostly used on ships that get a lot of exposure to water and salt, it hardly gets affected by those factors.

• Store the rope in a cool and dry place where it won't be destroyed by mold or rot.

• It is good for farming, landscape operations, exercises, suspension of items, decorations, and even fishing nets.

2. **Hemp**

- This rope is different from the manila rope. They are made from hemp plants.

- Even though they have tensile strength similar to manila, they have a smoother texture, almost like how linen feels when you touch it.

- It is mostly used by sailors for navigating the ship. To prevent it from being destroyed by mold or rot, you could rub tar all along the surface.

3. **Cotton**

- Ropes made out of this material are great for beginners as they are very easy to knot.

- They are smooth and soft to touch.

- The only issue with cotton ropes is that they don't stand the test of time. They are also prone to rotting quickly when exposed to certain elements like water.

4. **Sisal**

- This kind of rope looks just like twines.

- They are hard, coarse, and can stand the test of time because it has a small inner circle.

- Sisal can be used to make twines.

5. **Jute**

• Jute is another natural material used to make ropes.

• Ropes made from jute contain as much fiber as cotton ropes do.

• Jute ropes aren't too costly and they offer as much strength as you'd want them to offer.

• It is prone to rotting and easily grows weak when submerged in water.

Synthetic Rope Materials

When synthetic ropes were developed, natural ropes were used in lower quantities as the former had better qualities. They were stronger, and resistant to scratches, mildew, rots, molds, insects, and vermin. However, when it is wet, it begins to swell up and when it is dumped in cold areas, it freezes up so much that the fibers could snap into two.

So, most synthetic ropes have been streamlined to address industrial functions. Examples of such rope materials include nylon, polypropylene, and polyesters. The natural ones, on the other hand, have been left for decorative purposes. Now, let's look at each of the synthetic rope materials available and their downsides.

1. **Nylon**

• Nylon was the first synthetic material from which ropes were made from. It still remains the commonest material used for rope construction.

• Nylon is also known as a Polyamide.

• It has a great tensile strength, and it can stand the test of time.

• It becomes weak when submerged in water.

• This material is very good for dynamic climbing ropes as it has a bit of elastic properties that can absorb the energy stirred from a person's fall.

• It is used to anchor warps, two vehicles, and for climbing rocks.

• It is resistance to attack by acids, alkalis, oils, and other organic solvents.

2. **Polypropylene**

• This material is one of the few inexpensive ones that still offer a lot of great properties.

- They have a light weight that allows them to float easily on water and become highly resistant to mildew and rots.

- They do not absorb too much water, so they don't shrink much when they're wet.

- Because they don't get affected or deteriorated by water, they are employed for activities like water skiing.

- Polypropylene is dielectric, and so, it doesn't conduct electricity through its fibers. This particular feature allows it to be preferred by people working with electric poles, as they'd not get electrocuted.

- Polypropylene ropes are constructed from multifilament, monofilament, staple fiber, and split films.

- They have a breaking strength that's half that of nylon.

- They have a melting point that's much lower than that of nylon (around 150°C). Because of this low temperature, it is very useless for operations that generate a lot of heat due to friction.

- It is resistant to attack by acids, alkalis, oils, but then, not to bleaching agents.

- The cheap ones undergo denaturation when exposed to the sun.

3. **Polyethylene**

- This synthetic material also floats in water. This is one reason it is employed for activities like fishing and waterskiing that are done in areas with water.

- However, when compared to polypropylene, it does not offer as much abrasion resistance.

4. **Polyesters**

- Polyester is greater tensile strength than nylon when it is wet and a strength that's almost equal to nylon's when it is dry.

- They have a bit elastic properties that make them suitable for mountain climbers. In case the climber falls, the rope will be able to absorb the energy from the fall.

- They can be used during rigging operations.

- They are not susceptible to destruction from rots, sunlight, water, molds or any other physical element.

- Since polyesters can last long without losing their quality, they are used in marine activities. Although they often lose their coloration when they are exposed to water for long periods.

- Very similar in physical appearance to nylon, but then, it has only a few differences, of which resistance to chemicals is one.

- This material's tensile strength remains the same no matter the condition they are put under.

- They are sold under the brand names of Terylene and Dacron.

- Ropes made from this material can be used for rigging, sheets, halyards, etc.

5. **High-Tech Fibers**

- This material can be used to make ropes that are impermeable to bullets.

- The fibers being discussed here include Kevlar and polyethylene, which are a lot stronger than nylon. Kevlar is an organic polymer that is resistant to moisture and rot. There's also HPME (Spectra), which is light and with a tensile strength greater than that of stainless steel.

- High-tech fibers have only little elastic properties.

- These kinds of fibers are good for sailing as they are resistant to water.

- The only issue tied to this kind of rope is that they are very costly.

The other kinds of synthetic ropes are made from rayon and flexible metallic strips.

Rope Construction

Several steps are involved in making ropes from several base materials. These steps are grouped into the following. They are;

1. **Laid ropes**. When making laid ropes, you go by twisting fibers around each other. That is why they are also known as twisted ropes. These ropes are the commonest kinds of ropes made. To make laid ropes, you'd have to go through three major processes. The first stage involves rolling the fibers you'd use for the rope into yarns. After that, you'd twist the yarns to form major strands. The last stage involves rolling the strands into ropes. For the strands to stay fixed, the yarns are twisted in a direction opposite that of the strands. Then, the

direction in which the strands are twisted is opposite that in which the rope is twisted.

There are two types of twisted ropes. One is formed from three strands that are twisted around to form ropes. This type is the 3-strand twisted rope. The other type is the one formed from two pairs of ropes twisted headed in the right direction and another two pairs twisted in the left direction. It is referred to as the 8-strand twisted rope. When twisting strands, you could decide to either follow Z's or S's central line.

The ones that are laid in an 'S' pattern are referred to as left-laid ropes. The ones laid in a 'Z' pattern are called right-laid ropes. Twisted ropes have a few elastic properties and these things will be very useful for the anchorage of ships. Twisted ropes are also very easy to splice.

The only issue with twisted ropes is that their ends begin to untwist around their knots as you use them. And this can really be an issue if this kind of rope is used to keep an object in position.

2. **Braided ropes**. These kinds of ropes did not become the talk of the town until weaving and braiding machines were developed and introduced into the rope industry. There are different kinds of braided ropes, and there's one that comes in single braids. These ones have about eight to twelve strands that are weaved in the outline of circles. Half of the strands are weaved in a clockwise direction and the other half in the other direction. With this technique, you could easily create a rope with the look of a tube. They are durable and can be used with pulleys due to their exceptional ability to withstand pressure. Single braided ropes lack cores and are created by weaving the final strands.

   Double-braided ropes are also referred to as marine ropes. They have cores, i.e., middle layers and sheaths, i.e., outer layers. The strands of the sheath are usually weaved around the braided strands of the core. So, with this technique, you get a rope buried inside another rope, a vey strong structure. When talking about weight-bearing, the core and the sheath are both responsible. So, braided ropes are thicker, stronger, and offer many resistance to factors like scratches and jamming. They also keep their shapes as time runs.

Kernmantle ropes have many similarities to double-braided ropes, but then here, the core, known as the Kern, consists of twisted fibers that run in directions parallel to one another. These inner fibers are then wrapped with an outer sheath called mantle. The mantle works to protect the Kern from abrasion. The Kern, on the other hand, is what supplies the strength needed for Kernmantle ropes. This rope is used for climbing mountains, caves, trees, and for rescuing items from fire.

The Kernmantle rope has two forms. One is dynamic and it is the kind that is used for climbing up rocks. Why? The dynamic Kernmantle is one that has a lot of elasticity that must be shown by climbing ropes. So, in case the person climbing falls, it can help reduce the impact of the fall by using its elastic properties to take in the energy generated by the fall. This way, there is little possibility of the rope snapping along its length from the pull offered by the climber's weight. The second type is the static Kernmantle that isn't as elastic as the dynamic one.

3. **Plaited ropes.** Plaited ropes have a rough texture that is formed by weaving four twisted ropes into square braids. They don't have as much round shape as most twisted ropes and aren't susceptible to conditions like kinking, and jamming. Plaited ropes are flexible, easy to knot, and easy to operate upon.

4. **Endless winding ropes.** When you wound strands made from high-quality yarns in such a way that their two ends look uncompleted, you get endless winding ropes. You continue to wound the strands until you reach a point where they cannot break easily. These kinds of ropes don't have too many elastic properties though.

Choosing the Right Rope

When choosing a rope, you might want to consider if it can be gripped with no issue at all or not, if it's too stiff, slippery, or costly. All these factors vary with the purpose the rope is playing. Some ropes are perfect for beginners and some aren't. Some knotting processes require very costly ropes and some that do not. Although we have discussed rope materials in the previous section, however, we will be reiterating the different rope materials that are commonly used and the attributes each possesses to help you in your choice of rope.

Propylene

- This rope is a synthetic rope.
- It is a rope adapted for use in water.
- It is resistant to rotting caused by moisture and mildew.
- It is produced in several colors.
- Its ability to float makes it useful for the division of swimming pools into lanes.
- This rope can be used in making nets, crab lines, and other fishing equipment. It is also very useful in aquaculture.
- It's insulating properties makes it useful for electricians. So, in cases where the rope touches sites with electric current, it doesn't conduct it.
- It has a light weight.
- It is resistant to ultraviolet rays and heat.
- It has elastic properties and so, it is suitable for mountain climbers. However, once it stretches, it doesn't return back to its normal length.

- It is prone to friction. If you choose this rope for hauling objects, make sure that they don't rub against the ropes too much.
- It can used in the production of electric lines and swimming lanes.

Manila

- It has a natural tensile strength.
- It satisfies a lot of purposes and functions.
- It is completely made of hemp fibers.
- Its ornate look makes it suitable for decorative purposes and landscaping.
- This rope is prone to destruction by sunlight and water. It also cannot support too much load.
- Its ability to absorb water quickly makes it highly suitable for jobs or activities that require physical handling like tug-of-war and climbing. Your palms could get sweaty, but since the rope absorbs fluid quickly, you'd be able to grip it better and more tightly.
- This rope will not snap dangerously when broken or weak, unlike the other man-made ropes.
- They can be used as embellishments.

- It is not expensive.
- It is susceptible to damage by ultraviolet rays and water.
- This rope gets hardened as you use it.
- It can be used for rigging operations and for pulling objects.

Nylon

- It has a great strength.
- It has excellent elastic abilities and that makes it very suitable for activities related to climbing.
- It has a higher tensile strength than manila and polypropylene.
- It can be used to haul heavy weights or objects.
- It is resistant to scratches or consistent rubbing, so it is perfect for pulley systems.
- Nylon ropes are constructed in a way that counteracts the effects of falls.
- It gets weakened when left in water for long periods.
- It is one of the easiest ropes to find.
- Nylon melts at temperatures higher than 200°C and it could burn if subjected to more frictional forces.

- Nylon ropes are great or beginners to practice with.
- It's not too good for splicing because its fibers get easily disorganized, thereby making the end result an untidy look.
- This rope can be used for anchoring objects, in pulley systems, tie-downs and for fall protection.

Polyester

- It is used for several purposes.
- It is a heavy duty rope with a high tensile strength.
- It works well for rigging operations and any other outdoor activities. It is well adapted to fight against adverse weather conditions.
- It can be used to hold boats in place.
- Polyester can be used in pulley systems, winches, dock rigging, and a lot of other operations.
- Polyester is resistant to rot and ultraviolet rays. Also, whether it is wet or dry, it still retains its strength.
- It is resistant to consistent rubbing or abrasion.
- When used for marine operations, its white color changes to brown or green.

Kevlar

- It is resistant to water.
- It is resistant to ultraviolet light.
- It has a bullet proof structure.
- It is resistant to chemicals.
- It is resistant to fire.
- It is resistant to freezing conditions.
- It is stronger than stainless steel.
- It doesn't get rusted.
- It can be used in oil rigs and in ships.
- It is expensive.
- In activities where a lot of balance is required, go for this rope as it has little to no elastic properties.

Apart from the ropes listed above, it is important to note a few other things. Twisted ropes, because of their spiral forms, prevent the rope from unwinding from its knots. They are also relatively easy to splice. Braided ropes have a rounded form and smooth texture that makes it suitable for operations where a lot of friction is generated like in pulley systems.

You should also know that the tensile strength of ropes reduce at high temperatures. And if the ropes are continuously exposed to external factors continuously, they could get damaged permanently.

To make a 3-strand eye splice, you need a 3-strand twisted rope. To make a Brummel splice, you need a rope with a hollow braid. To make a beer knot, you need a rope with tubular webbings.

As a beginner, search for a rope that you can easily untie its knots. It will also help if the rope is flexible, and not too shiny or slippery. You need not worry much about its tensile strength since you wouldn't be starting with big projects like oil rigging. You should try to stay away from polypropylene ropes as they aren't all that great to handle. The knots tied on them do not last for long too. Avoid getting too expensive and high-tech ropes since these ones are for big projects. Avoid getting ropes that are bulky with large diameters. Stick with thin braided threads like ones of ¼ inches diameter. Bear at the back of your mind that ropes made from natural materials can knot easily. They are also good for splicing as they retain their original form.

Lastly, we'll see some basic operations and what kind of rope material is good for them.

1. **Knot tying:** For this operation, use nylon ropes. Nylon ropes have man-made fibers that will work brilliantly for basic knots. You could actually use any

kind of rope for knots, but then, a lot of them are usually too stiff and stretchy. If you need to make complex knots, use manila ropes. They retain the shape of knots and can be used to teach people the principles of making knots. Try not to use polypropylene for knot tying.

2. **For outdoor activities**: Polyester and manila ropes are the best for outdoor activities. They are resistant to ultraviolet light, can stand the test of time, are not destroyed by water, knot easily, and most importantly, retain their strength even with time. If you have to go hiking, use the rope options given above. Do not risk using Kevlar rope.

3. **Dock lines**: Dock lines help connect a boat to a dock or to another boat. They could be either permanent or temporary. Nylon ropes are the best for this purpose. Dock lines require strong ropes that have elastic properties and are capable of taking in shock well enough. For this purpose, do not work with sisal ropes.

4. **Tie-downs**: Tie-downs are used to hold boats to poles and most times, this process occurs outdoor. So, the vest rope for tie-downs is the nylon rope. It can stretch and still remain as strong as ever. It is also resistant to ultraviolet light and chemicals. When exposed to water, nylon ropes could lose their strength, but it does so in little percentages. For less stretch and increased strength of nylon ropes, use ¼ inches of four braided strands. Do not use polypropylene for this activity.
5. **Towing vehicles and other objects**: Use nylon ropes for this process. Remember that towing a vehicle requires using a strong rope that is equally dense and receptive to shock waves. For this process, do not use polypropylene, manila or cotton ropes.
6. **Flagpoles**: Polyester ropes are the best for flagpoles. They have low stretching abilities and are heavily resistant to ultraviolet rays and abrasion. If you are working with a 40ft pole, use

a 80ft polyester rope with a diameter of either ⅓ inches or ⅝ inches.

7. **Macramé**: For this activity, make use of cotton ropes. This activity will require a lot of physical handling, so you need something that will not tear open your palms. Do not use polypropylene or sisal ropes for this purpose.
8. **Resistance to ultraviolet rays:** If you need a rope with this kind of resistance, work with polyester ropes. Stay away from cotton and polypropylene ropes as they aren't suitable for outdoor projects.
9. **Clothesline**: Use polyester. It is strong, durable, and resistant to ultraviolet rays. Do not use polypropylene ropes.
10. **Non-stretching ropes**: The best rope to use here is the synthetic rope, Kevlar. If it is going to be used outdoors, it'd be great if it was reinforced with polyester fibers so that it can last longer. Do not use polypropylene or nylon ropes to fill in for this need.
11. **Stretching ropes**: Polypropylene is the best rope for this purpose. Work with a solid fiber braid or

twisted rope to solve the issue of pressure and to last long for outdoor purposes. Do not use Kevlar or polyester for this need.

12. **Farming**: Use polyester ropes for this need. They are strong with nice elastic abilities. You can also tie and untie knots easily with this kind of rope. Use solidly braided polyester ropes for this purpose. Do not use polypropylene ropes here.

13. **Marine operations**: The best rope for this need is the polyester rope. They don't shrink when water touches them. They are also resistant to ultraviolet light, mold, chemicals, and moisture. They aren't too costly either.

14. **Tree swings**: Use Polyester ropes for tree swings. They are suitable for outdoor uses and have enough resistance to adverse physical factors. Do not use manila ropes or propylene for tree swings.

15. **Fencing**: Use manila rope for fencing. Stay away from polypropylene.

Choosing the Right Knot

The difference between most of the knots available today is the difference in their strengths. This factor is one most mountain climbers consider as their weight exerts a lot of downward pressure on the knots. So, if it is too weak, it could loosen, which could be dangerous to their lives. That is one big reason why climbers use bulky knots made with a lot of turnings and tucking. You might also want to consider how easy it is to tie a knot and, afterward, loosen it. Is it something you can do very quickly with your eyes closed or not?

Another thing to consider when choosing a knot is its ability to absorb pressure from weight and jarring. Most knots end up weakening ropes, so you need to be sure that you choose the right one. How flexible is your rope? Rigid ones are usually difficult to knot, and so, the knot you eventually get may become very insecure and loose, which can be very dangerous to your life. Let's see a few of the thousand knots that can be tied and then decide if it's right for you.

Square knots

- These knots are easy to knot and unknot.

- With square knots, you can join two ropes in a simple fashion.
- Do not use this kind of knot to drag or suspend heavy weights.
- This knot is what you would need when holding the ends of a bandage or tying your shoelaces.
- To use this knot, you might need a few skills.
- Square knots are effective in fishing, hunting, lashing, boating, and several other purposes.

Bowline knots

- This knot is mostly used in marine areas.
- It is useful for a whole lot of operations.
- It is simple to knot, unknot, tie and isn't prone to jamming.
- Once you tie this knot, you would get an open loop that allows you the grace to hang the knot on a post.
- This knot doesn't loosen if you shake it.
- It is perfect for sailing and for safety measures.

Overhand knot

- It is a simple knot.

- To tie this kind of knot are the most basic steps ever.
- When climbing ropes, you can use this knot as a stopper. It also helps to prevent ropes from slipping out of a pulley system.
- This knot is good for lashing the ends of a rope and preventing fraying issues.

Slip knot

- This knot helps to tighten a knot around a tree or post.
- It can tighten easily even when it is bearing a lot of weight.
- It works as a noose, i.e., one side of it gets smaller as you pull at one of the ends of the rope involved in making that knot.
- It is great for camping, stopping, and holding.

Weaver's knot

- This knot is also known as the sheet bend knot.
- You can use this knot to join to ropes of unequal sizes and dimensions.
- It can be used for broken splices.

- It is good for hunting, camping, temporary stoppage, and all sorts of general uses.

Single knots

- This knot is also known as the overhand knot, and it is one of the most elementary knots known in history.
- It is used to prevent materials like cotton, threads, or strings from fraying at the edges.
- This is the knot you tie when you want to prevent a piece of thread from slipping out of a needle hole.

Overhand knots with draw loop

- This knot is good in a case where you need to quickly untie it.
- It helps to strengthen a knot by adding weight to it.

Two strand overhand knots

- This knot is bigger and used for stopping the ends of bulky materials.
- It can be used for cotton ropes and strings.

- You can use this knot to join two cords together. Just make sure they lie in the same direction.

Double overhand knots

- This knot is even bigger than the overhand knot.
- Other knots are based upon this knot

Triple and multiple overhand knots

- To get this kind of knot, all you need to do is tuck in the working end into the loop three times.
- It can be used to shorten ropes and for embellishments.
- This knot is what you would see around the waists of nuns.

Strangle knot

- This knot is usually tied around a pole or stick
- You can use this knot to prevent the cut ends of a rope from fraying.
- You can use this knot to keep a roll of carpet in place.

Tips and Techniques of Tying a Rope Knot

When tying a rope knot, a few tips listed here will help you get it right.

- Start with simple knots before proceeding on to the tough ones.
- Practice making knots as often as possible.
- Before cutting through a rope, use tape to hold down the edge, not to get subject to fraying.
- When tying the knots, go slowly to make sure you do not miss any step.

Now, for the techniques, we will look at some of them that will serve as a base for what you ought to practice.

Simple, overhand knot

- Form an overhand loop in the rope material you want to tie.
- Tuck the rope's running end through the loop you formed above and then, tighten the knot formed with the standing end.

Overhand knot with draw loop

- Form an overhand loop in the rope material.

- Pass the rope's working end through the loop formed, but here, make sure you don't totally pull out the working end.

Two-strand overhand knot

- Place the two strings that you want to knot together in a direction parallel to each other.
- Tie a simple overhand knot.
- Tighten the knot while ensuring that the ropes or strings are still in a direction parallel to each other.

Double-overhand knot

- Tie an overhand knot, but see that the working end is tucked into the loop a second time.
- Pull the two ends of the rope in a direction away from each other while making sure to twist them in opposite directions. Your left thumb should go in an upward direction that is away from you. Keep your right thumb down and away from you.

Triple overhand knots

- Tie a double overhand knot and then tuck the running end a third time through the loop.
- Tug at both ends of the rope tightly while rotating the ends in different directions that will stir a diagonal wrapping turn.

Strangle knot

- Start out with a double overhand knot, but make sure you keep the knots loose.
- Fix in the end of the rope you want to keep in place while ensuring that the diagonal lines stay on top of the other two parts of the knot.
- Tighten the knot by pulling the two ends of the loop tightly.

Single hitch

- Tie the overhand knot around a rod.
- Make sure that the working end is longer and does not totally come out through the draw loop.

Two half hitches

- Tie a single half hitch with the rope's working end.

- Join a second half hitch similar to the first one and then, pull them tightly together to finish this knot.

Round turn and two half hitches

- Pass the running end of the rope around the side that anchors the knot. This point should be about the standing side of the rope. Make this knot a half hitch.
- Make another hitch similar to the first one to finish this knot.

Overhand knot and half hitch

- Tie an overhand knot with a large draw loop and then shift the loop to the size you need by pulling one of the ends of the rope.
- Wrap half of the hitch with the working end, wound about the standing end.
- Tighten the knot by pulling each end of the loop one by one.

Overhand loop

- Fold one end of the rope into two and make a loop with that doubled end.
- With that end, tie an overhand knot while ensuring that the ends of the knot are kept in a parallel line. Tighten the knot the rope forms by pulling on either of the ends of the knots one by one.

Double overhand loop

- Make a long bight and then, with that, tie a double overhand knot.
- If there are any parts of the knot that came out uncrossed, pull out the slack until the knot goes back to its original shape. From there, tighten the knot gradually while pulling slowly at each end of the knot.

Surgeon's loop

- Make a long bight and then tie an overhand knot that goes in the shape of a treble clef.
- Cancel out the uneven knots and use your fingers to make a knot shaped into the form of a barrel.

You can rub a little fluid on the rope to lubricate it as it moves.

Simple noose

- Tie an overhand knot while making sure to move your fingers away from the short end of the rope. Ensure that the knot you tie has a draw loop attached to it.
- Pull the ends of the rope strongly to form a tight knot.

Scaffold knot

- Form a bight with the rope and tie a double overhand knot with the lead's working end.
- Pull the end of the rope and the other end forming the loop in opposite directions to tighten the knot.

Overhand bend

- Tie an overhand knot in the end of one of the two lines you join. In that knot, tuck in the end of the second line.

- With the original knot taking the base, pass the second running end through the knot.
- If the knot is meant to occur in two folds, see that all the parts of the knot involved are parallel to each other and that the rope's short ends come out at the top of the knot. With this technique, you can get a knot that comes out stronger. To tighten this knot, pull the standing parts close together.

Fisherman's knot

- Arrange the two strings in a direction parallel to each other with one end going around the standing part of the other string.
- Turn the half-completed knot's end and then, tie an overhand knot that is similar to it with the other end of the rope. Pull the two working ends to see that each knot is tightened. Then, to tighten the whole knot, pull on the standing parts.

Double Fisherman's knot

- Place the two strings of rope parallel to each other with little to no distance between them. Tie a

double overhand knot with one working end wound around the other standing end.
- Turn the half-completed knot to its end before making a second double overhand knot with the other end. Before you pull the standing parts towards each other in an attempt to close the knot, first fix each knot.

Multiple scaffold knot

- Tie a simple triple overhand knot with the running end around the standing end of the rope.
- Tug at each end of the rope and the leg of each loop in opposite directions to tighten the knots.

Flemish bend

- Form a loop with one end of the two strings you want to join.
- Form half of a twist, with your left thumb going up and away from you, mimicking an anticlockwise move.
- Pass the working end of the rope to create the outline of figure eight.

- Pass a second string through the loop with the working end parallel to the first string.
- Work along with the first string with the second string. Make sure that you keep the string moving towards the outer edge of the first bend.
- Continue with the original knot while transferring the first rope to the inner whorls of the second rope.
- Finish the knot before tightening it slowly by tugging slowly on each working end before moving to the standing edge.

Double figure-of-eight bend

- Tie a figure-eight knot in one of the two strings and then fix the second string through the first knot.
- Tie another figure-eight knot.
- Finish the second figure-eight knot so that it is similar to the first one.
- Tug on the working ends of the rope to get rid of the slack from each knot. Then, tug on the two standing parts to slide them together.

Linfit knot

- Form a bight with each of the two strings that you want joined before you lay them on top of each other.
- Use the upper rope's working end to pass across the lower rope's back, starting from the left to the right.
- Pass the lower rope's working end across the upper rope, starting from the left to the right.
- Move the left working end through a clockwise direction while making a pass around the standing end at the left.
- Tuck the working end at the left from behind and pass it through the bight to the left side.
- Pass the working end towards the right in an anticlockwise direction while moving across the standing part to the right.
- Pass the working end from the front in a downward direction through the right side's bight. You can get rid of the slack until you get something symmetrical with both of its ends at

right angles to the standing ends. Make sure they are positioned on the same side of the knot.
- Tug on each working and standing end to tighten the completed knot.

Zeppelin bend

- Hold two ropes together with their ends heading towards the same direction.
- Form a loop with the running end closer to you.
- Pass that working end behind both ropes and then pass it back through its loop.
- Take up the standing part of the other loop and move it towards its working end.
- Pass the second rope's working end under its standing part and then tuck it through the newly formed loop. Tug at both working and standing ends to eradicate any slack and to tighten the knot.

Adjustable bend

- Lay the two lengths of the string parallel to each other. Wrap one of the strings around the other whilst moving towards its nearest end.

- With the first string, make a second turn around the second string.
- Move the working end around and under the wrapped string within its standing end.
- Move the working end to the front of the second line before tucking it under the final turn.
- Turn the half-completed knot towards the end with the second string to make a second knot that is identical to the first one.

Hunter's bend

- Arrange the two strings that you want to join in a direction in which they are parallel to each other.
- With the two strings, make two loops that are similar to each other while ensuring that the two strings remain parallel.
- Pass the working end from the front of the loop all the way to the back.
- Tuck that end from the back to the front of both loops.
- Pass the other working end up from a direction right from the front of the loops.

- Tuck the working end through the loop from the front to the back, in a direction that is opposite to the first end.
- Remove the slack from the knot while ensuring that the working ends don't come out of the loops.
- Tug at each working end and the standing end one by one until the knot is tight enough.

Pedigree cow hitch

- Take the working end around the rod and down while moving from the front to the back of the anchor point.
- Take the end around the rod and bring it to the front of its standing part.
- Take the end of the rope back up from behind the foundation and then bring it down in front again.
- Tuck the end of the rope through the bight to get the common cow hitch.
- Tuck the working end of the rope back through the knot to keep it tight in place.

Cow hitch variant

- Pass the working end of the rope around the rod.
- Form a single half hitch with the working end around the standing part of the line.
- Take the working end away from the front and pass it up from the back of the anchor point.
- Take the working end down from the front of the knot and then tuck it back beside the standing part of the line. Then, take it pass the turn that encloses the knot.

Figure-of-eight hitch

- Pass the working end of the rope around the anchor line from the front of the rod to the back.
- Take the end forward and across the rope's standing part. Go from the right direction to the left.
- Take the end of the rope from the left to the right side and then move around to the back of the standing part.
- Tuck the end up through the loop to form that characteristic figure-of-eight layout.

Buntline hitch

- Pass the working end of the rope around the rod. Go round the anchor point and move from the front to the back.
- Take the end across the front of the rod and then, pass it around its back in a figure of eight layout.
- Pass the end completely over the loop that has been created.
- Continue taking the end to the back of the knot.
- Tuck the working end from the back of the knot to the front to form two half hitches.

Clove hitch

- Make an overhand loop at any position in the line.
- Make an underhand loop as you go down the line so that the two come out as opposing halves.
- Set the two loops such that they have the same size and are packed tightly together.
- Turn the loops in an opposite direction in a way that they can overlap.
- Fix in a rail through the loops to either loosen or tighten the final hitch.

Common whipping

- Create a long bight with one rope and fix it to the other side of another rope string.
- Roll the working end of the first rope about the rope while ensuring that both of its ends are tucked into the bight. When rolling the working end in, do them in the opposite direction. This will go a long way to tighten the whipping's knot.
- Continue to roll the working end while moving towards the outer edge of the second rope. Ensure that none of the wrap moves overlaps the other. This technique will help you get neat lines. You should only stop winding the rope about the second one when the windings are as long as the rope's radius.
- Tuck the rope's working end through the rest portion of the bight.
- Tug at the rope's working end to reduce the bight of rope formed. Do this step until the rope's running edge is trapped into place. This step is over when the elbows get to the whipping's middle. Then, trim the ends.

Perfected whipping

- Arrange the ends of a whipping string closely together, making sure that their heads are pointing towards opposite directions.
- Start to wrap a string of rope around the rope from one part of the rope to the other.
- Ensure that you wrap the twines very tightly while ensuring to keep the underlying parts parallel and close together. Untangle the running end from the rope's end.
- As the working bight of the rope shrinks, get rid of that twist that is tied to it. As you practice though, you should fix in a twist that runs in the counterclockwise direction.
- Tug on the twine's end to get rid of all the slack from the final wrapping. After that, you can then pull tightly on both ends of the knots to tie the knot in place.

West country whipping

- Make an overhand knot that is about 2.5 cm from one of the ends of the rope.

- With the rope turned with its front down, make an identical second overhand knot on the other side.
- Ensure that the side of the rope you are working on is facing upwards before you tie a third overhand knot. Do this procedure continuously at either of the sides.
- End the process with a square knot, and then poke back at the ends of the rope under the finished whipping with a pointed edge tool.

Sail maker's whipping

- Untwist one of the ends of the rope until you've gone through a distance of 5cm. Then, pass the whipping twine's bight over one strand so that both ends of the twine come out from the other two strands.
- Rearrange the strands before choosing any end of the rope with which you start whipping.
- Wrap the twine neatly towards the end of the rope.

- Continue with the wrapping until its length is as long as the rope's diameter.
- Arrange the rope's bight so that it spirals with one of its ends lining each groove formed by the original strand.
- Make a loop with the bight over the strand and then tug at it tightly with the twine's standing end.
- Set the twine's end in the same helix as the third groove.
- Knot both ends tightly in a position that lies in between the strands, using a square knot.

How to Untie Rope Knots
1. To untie large knots that are stiff, you could lightly tap the knot with a hammer.
2. Find the knot's loop and try to loosen it with the aid of your fingers.
3. You can choose to loosen loops by rolling one end of the rope and forcing it through the knot's loop.
4. Use devices such as corkscrew, skewer, and so on to tug at the knot.

5. Use tools like needles, pliers, and forceps to push the knot apart. Ensure that you tug at the rope gently to prevent the rope from snapping.
6. Twist one end of the rope in a clockwise direction to loosen the knot. The tighter the knot is, the more you need to turn the rope.
7. Immerse the knot in water. This technique is good for materials made from fiber and other water-absorbing materials.
8. If the knot is so strong that none of the methods above work for it, you can cut it with a pair of scissors or a blade.
9. Do not untie wet ropes. Dry knots are easier to unknot.
10. To know the area where you need to tug the knot, find the side that is a bit mobile about its center.

Rope Knot Safety Procedures

There are several rope knot safety procedures to be observed when dealing with ropes and knots. Some of them include the following;

1. Store your ropes in a place where they won't cause you to trip and fall.
2. When making knots, do the simplest ones. You should also work with ropes that will not scratch your fingers. For this reason, you should go for ropes of high quality. Sometimes, it is the cheap rope that people get that exposes them to hazard.
3. To prevent your rope from becoming prone to rot and mold, make sure it is kept dry at all times.
4. Certain chemicals have the power to cause ropes to grow rotten or weak. So, make sure that you keep your ropes in safe places where they cannot come in contact with harmful chemicals.
5. Note that heat and cold can destroy the materials used in the construction of ropes. So, it is important that you store your ropes under room temperature so that they don't grow weak.
6. When working with ropes, do not wound the extra strings around any part of your body as that can bring you harm. Instead, roll the strings around rods and sticks.

7. To prevent your ropes from getting all tangled up, keep your ropes in coiled forms. This technique will also prevent you from tripping over them when you move into your workshop.
8. Before you tie knots on ropes meant to bear the weights of people, ensure that you test the rope well before using it.
9. Before you tie a knot, make sure that you know completely the things each tool is used for.
10. Keep your ropes clean by washing them with soapy solutions or some special rope cleansers. If your ropes are exposed to salt water or marine areas, you might need to follow this technique.
11. You should always see that you check out a rope's breaking strength before using it. The load a rope should bear must not be more than 1/15 of its strength.
12. Note that knots reduce the strength possessed by ropes by a percentage of 50. This number causes the rope to begin to cut into their fibers.
13. Ensure that you do not connect ropes through sharp edges like roofs because there could be a

case of continuous abrasion that could lead to the rope snapping into two.

14. You should stop using a rope when it gets deteriorated by constant abrasion.
15. Note that ropes made from polyamide (nylon) will lose about 10% of its strength when it is wet.
16. You need to know the ropes you use well and their limitations.
17. Replace any rope whose working ability you doubt.

Caring for Your Rope Knots

1. Wash your ropes after using them each time.
2. You should protect your knots from the ultraviolet rays to prevent them from being destroyed by it.
3. Keep your rope knots free from kinks, knots, and twists.
4. There are small particles like crystals on the ground, so you should ensure that you do not stack your ropes on the ground.

5. Keep your rope knots from oxidizing agents, reducing agents, acids, alkalis, chemicals, and bleach.
6. To prevent dirt from getting into the core of your rope, do not place it somewhere that your feet will be able to match it.
7. For ropes made from materials like nylon, polyethylene, or polyester, you can shield their ends by melting them with a soldering iron.
8. Whip and apply heat to the ends of all your ropes.
9. For high-tech ropes like Kevlar, burning the ends may not do anything. If the rope is sheathed, it could melt and form a plastic covering around the core. To finish ropes like these, it's better if you use whippings for their ends. Make sure the length of the core is shorter than that of the sheath. After all that, you can now burn the sheath to keep the core enclosed.
10. If you are working with synthetic ropes, ensure that they are protected from anything that will generate heat or friction.

11. Do not allow wet ropes to get frozen.
12. Store your rope knots in places with humidity ranging between 40 and 60 percent.

A Short message from the Author:

Hey, I hope you are enjoying the book? I would love to hear your thoughts!

Many readers do not know how hard reviews are to come by and how much they help an author.

I would be incredibly grateful if you could take just 60 seconds to write a short review on Amazon, even if it is a few sentences!

>> Click here to leave a quick review

Thanks for the time taken to share your thoughts!

Chapter 4

Everyday Knot Tying Projects

Barrel Sling

You can use the knotted ropes here to lift or lower barrels. The working end of this rope is usually secured to the standing part of the rope.

Procedures

1. Pass the rope you want to use as a sling under the bottom of the bucket. Then, tie a half knot at the top of the barrel.

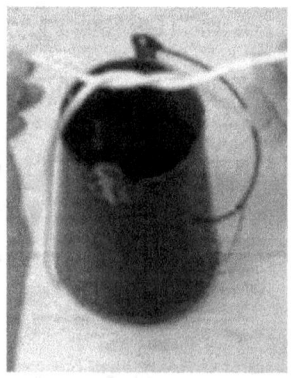

2. Divide the half knot into two and then make each knot part down over the load.

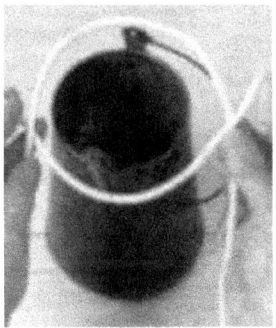

3. Tug upon both ends of the rope involved in making the knots at the two sides of the barrel.

4. Tie a bowline in the shorter end of the rope to the standing part. You are done.

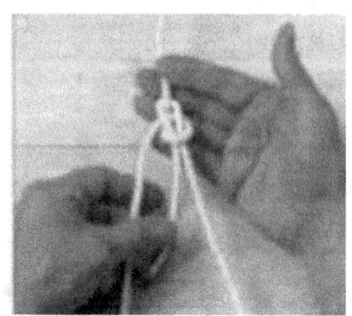

Plank Sling

Plank slings are usually constructed with ropes, not cords. It can be used to lift pieces of plank.

Procedures

1. Pass one end of the rope under the plank.

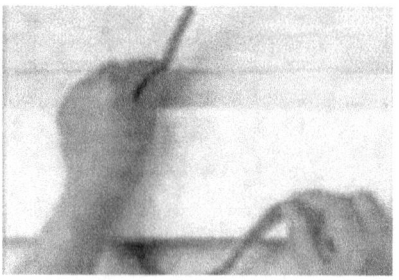

2. Pass a bight under that same plank while ensuring that the rope forms an 'S' or 'Z' shape.

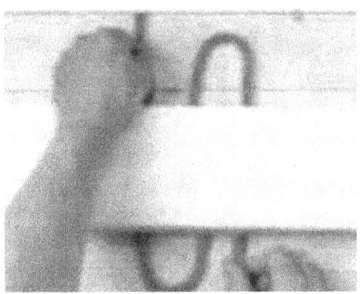

3. Pass one end of the rope over the surface of the plank. Then, you can push it through the bight just on the other side of the plank.

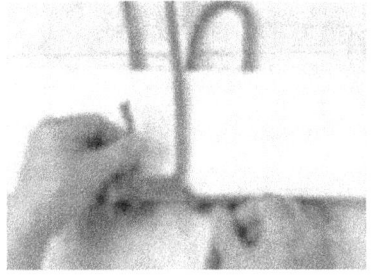

4. Pass the other end of the rope across the plank, but then pass it through the bight opposite it.

5. Tighten the sling so much that the tips of the bight you formed just hover above the corners of the plank. Tie the shorter end of the rope to the rope's standing part.

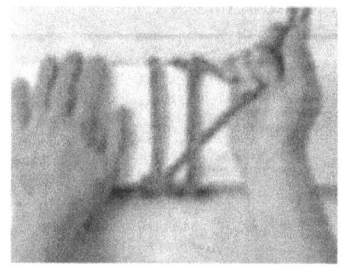

Jury Mast Knot

This knot has three loops you can easily adjust. It works to rig masts in boats.

Procedures

1. Cast the overhand loop in a clockwise direction through the rope's bight.

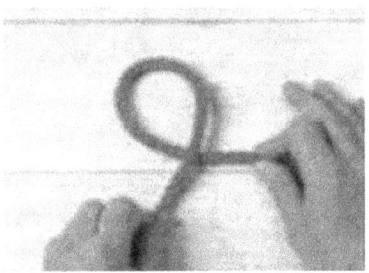

2. Add another underhand loop in a counterclockwise direction and see that the two loops overlap.

3. Form another counterclockwise underhand loop to the right of the other loops you already formed. Then, make sure it laps the center loop. Both loops should overlap the central loop.

4. Lap the left and right-hand loops over the central loop some more.

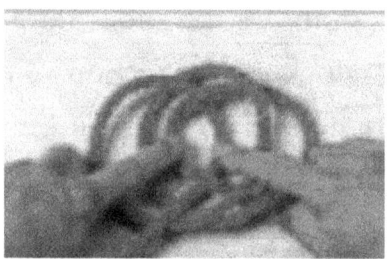

5. Pass the topmost part of the loop at the right under the loops to form a loop displaced towards the left.

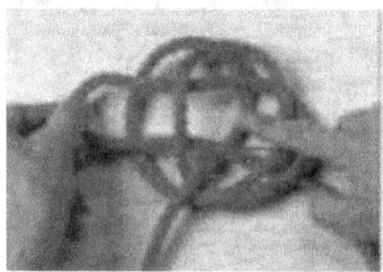

6. Pass the topmost part of the loop towards the left side under the loops to form a matching loop to the right.

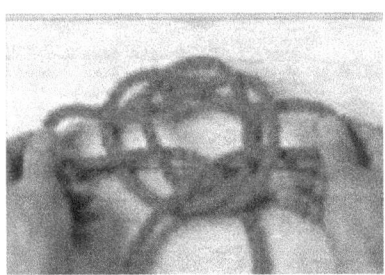

7. Lastly, push the upper edge of the central loop to form a third loop towards the top.

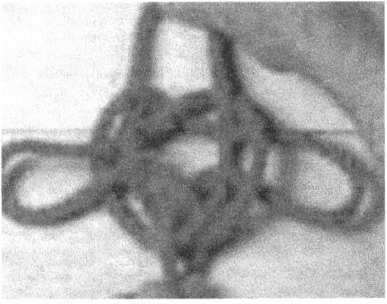

Three-Way Sheet Bend
This type of knot is useful for divers.

Procedures

1. Align three pieces of rope and they don't have to have identical sizes or textures.

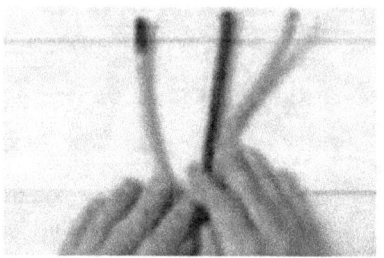

2. Form a bight in one of the pieces of the rope. You should use the larger and more rigid rope for this bight.

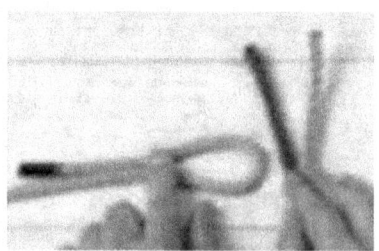

3. Pass the other two ends of the rope through the bight formed.

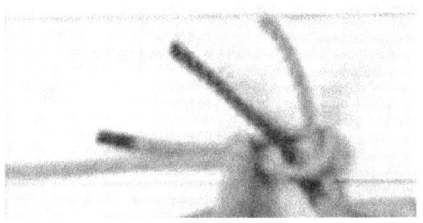

4. Wrap the two ropes about the bight you formed and then push them under themselves. This way, you can ensure that the running ends are on the same side as the finished knot.

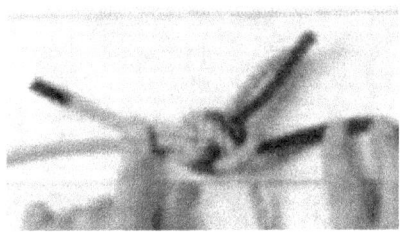

Poldo Tackle

This type of knot is good for clothesline.

Procedures

1. At one end of the rope, tie a strong and tight loop.

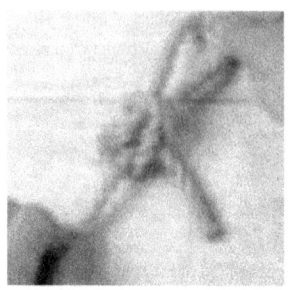

2. Push in the other end of the rope through the small loop you created above to form a larger running loop.

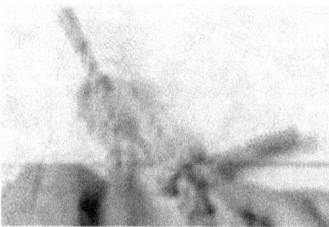

3. On the running leg of the large loop, make a sliding bight and gather the end around.

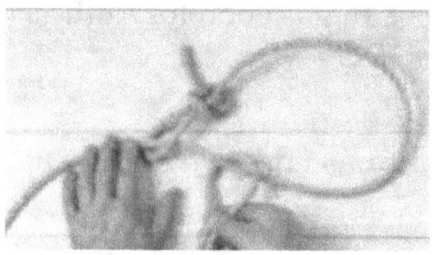

4. Keep the bight in place with a matching fixed loop knot. If you want to exact pressure on it, tug gently on the knots, with your hands going in opposite directions. If you want to reduce the pressure exacted on the knot, bring your hands back together to loosen it.

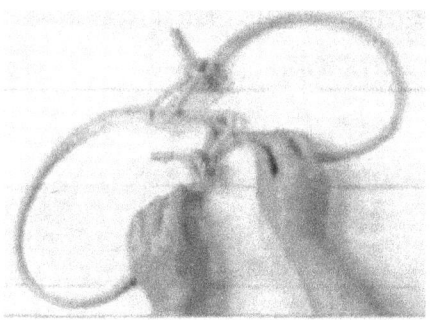

Chain Stitch Lashing

This knot is used for wrapping gift boxes and cartons.

Procedures

1. Tie a small loop at one end of the rope you use. From there, form a bight from the standing part of the rope.

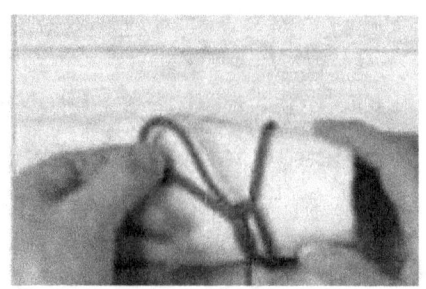

2. Take the rope's standing end far away from the bight while moving the rope up and behind the object you want to box.

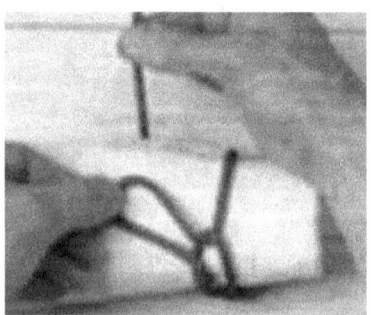

3. From the standing part, make a second bight down through the first bight you made

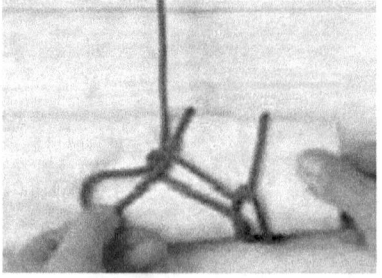

4. Pass the standing end away from the bight you just made and then pass it behind the parcel. From there, make a third bight from the same standing part and go up the second bight.

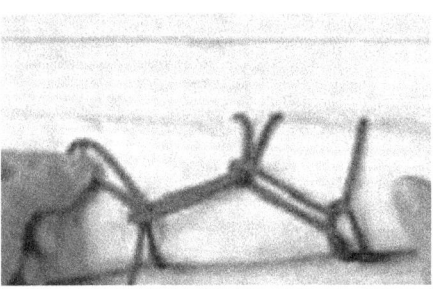

5. Repeat the second and third procedures while forming the fourth bight through the third bight.

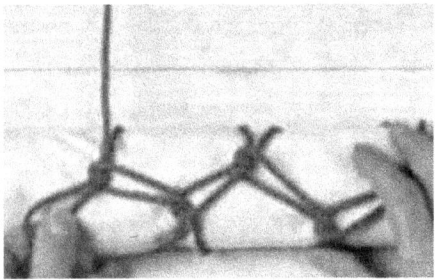

6. Interlace the opposite bights until you get to the end of the parcel. From there, pull out the running end totally through the last bight.

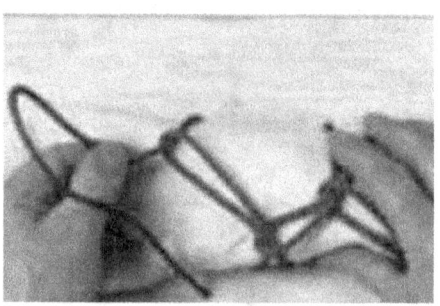

7. Pass the working end around the parcel once before you tuck it beneath the parcel.

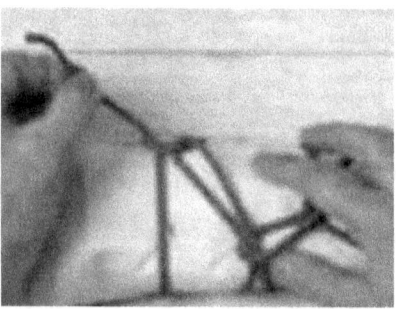

8. To secure the knots you have made, pass the working end around its standing end.

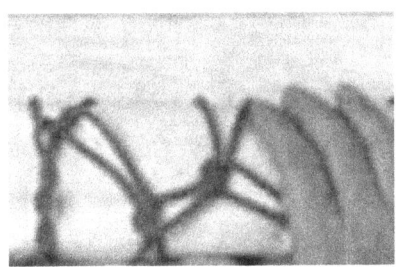

Half Hitching

This kind of knot is used to wrap long parcels.

Procedures

1. Make a sliding loop about the long parcel. Start from a small fixed loop and see that the long end is passed through it.

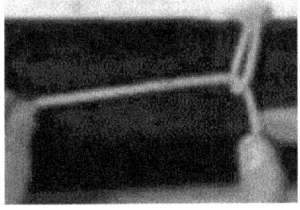

2. Make a clockwise underhand loop and tie it in the bight.

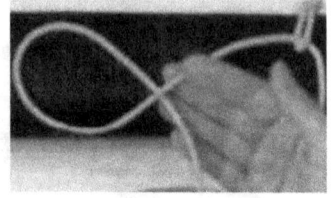

3. Pass the loop over the end of the long parcel before pulling the half hitch that is formed tightly.

4. Continue to add a series of half hitches, tie it in the bight, and then tighten them down so that the hitches are in line with one another and at the same distance apart.

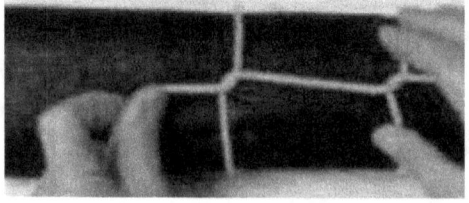

5. Flip the parcel and when you get to its end, which is at the first crossing point, make a crossing knot.

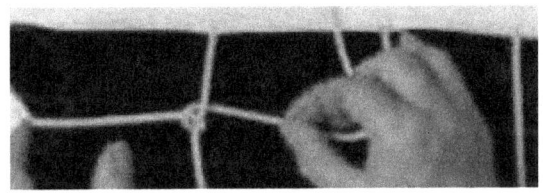

6. Add more of such crossing knots while applying the right pressure on each one to keep the space between the original half hitches constant.

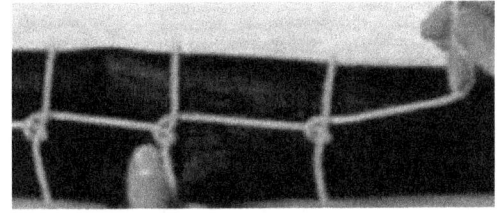

7. Go back to the other end of the parcel and then tie off the first small loop you made.

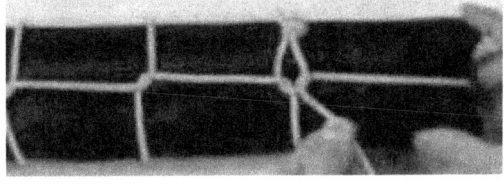

8. Finish your project by tying the knot with a couple of half hitches.

Marline Hitching

This knot is used to bundle carpets and rugs.

Procedures

1. Start your project with a sliding noose tied around the carpet. Tie a small fixed loop first before passing a running end through it.

2. With the working end, tie an overhead knot about the fold of carpet.

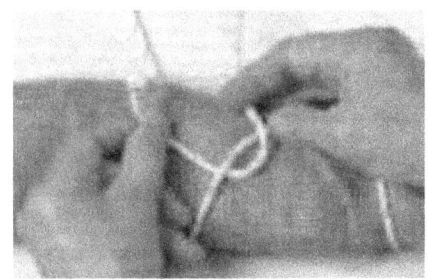

3. Tug at the ends of the knot to make the overhand knot tight. Unlike the normal hitching, there's an extra friction offered that will hold the other knots in place.

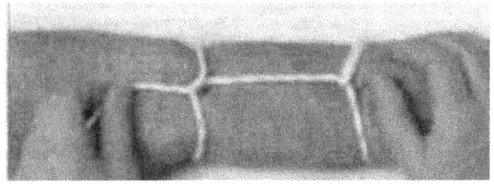

4. Add more of the overhand knots, with each spaced evenly along the length of the carpet.

5. Flip the carpet to the other side and go back to the point where you started with the crossing

knots. Then, tie it off to finish the knot and to make it firmer.

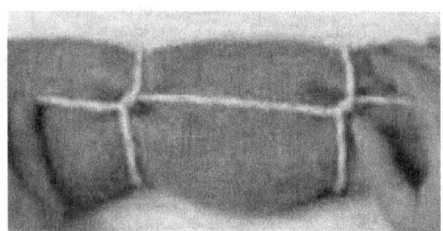

Diamond Hitch

This knot is good for travelers with backpacks that have some items they cannot pack into bags.

Procedures

1. Choose the right length that will work for lashing your backpack.

2. Fasten the standing end of the string to an anchor point placed at the central position.

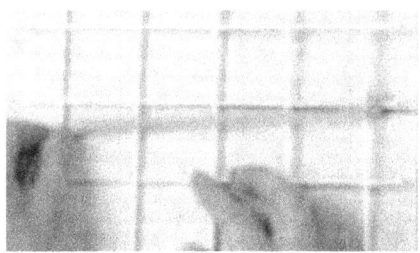

3. Move the string loosely across the load before moving on to the second anchor point that is opposite the first one. Then, you can return to the point you were coming from.

4. Turn the two parts of the lashing knot until you see a lot of its slack tightened. Then, find the central point of the twist.

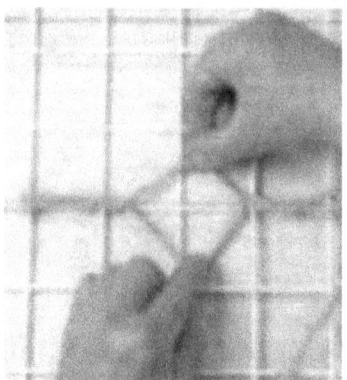

5. Pass the string down and around the lashing at the corner before going back to tuck it through the nearest central edge of the twisted part of the lashing.

6. Pass the line down around the next anchor corner.

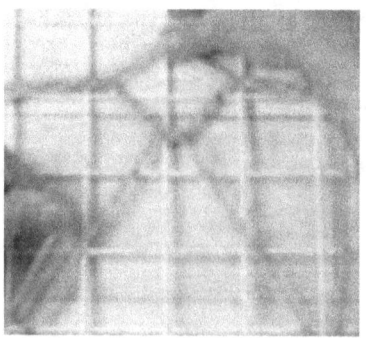

7. Bring up the string through the central diamond. This diamond is the reason this knot is called the diamond hitch.

8. Take the string around the third anchor point before bringing it back to tuck it again through the diamond at the center.

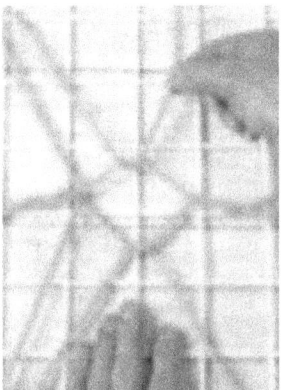

9. Pass the line around the rest of the anchor centers before bringing it down to the point you started. Tie the knot at this point.

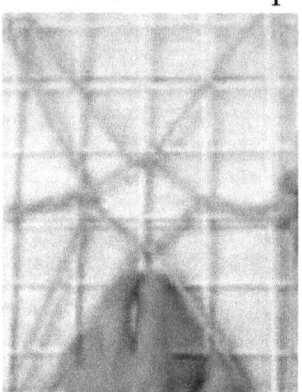

Trucker's Hitch

Truck drivers can use this knot to secure their goods safely to the back of their vehicle. It was formerly known as the wagoner's hitch.

Procedures

1. Fix the lashing to the anchor point at the farthest side of the vehicle. After that, you can pass the rope over the load.

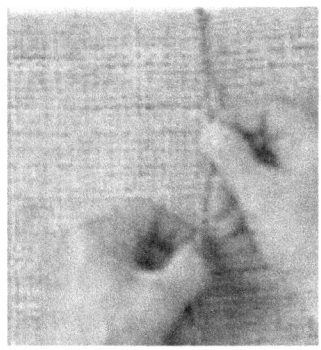

2. Make an overhand loop in the anticlockwise direction.

3. Make a bight in the standing part of the rope before tucking it from the back to the front side through a loop that was formed beforehand.

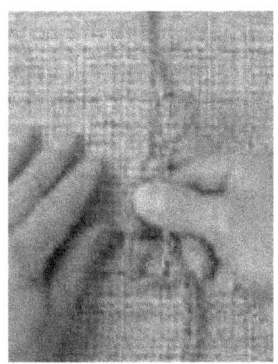

4. Make a half twist in an anticlockwise direction in the long loop created through the tucked bight.

5. Add one more half twist by forming two interlocked elbows in the lower loop.

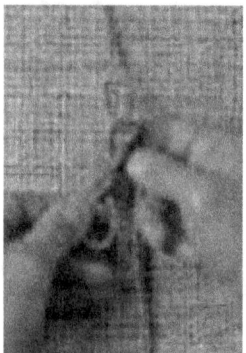

6. Get another bight from the standing part of the rope. This time, see that the bight is brought through the twisted lower loop.

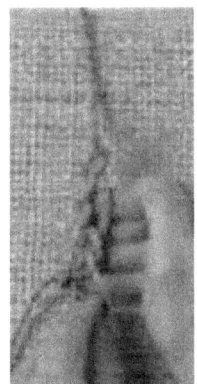

7. Pass the lower loop over an anchor point on a side of the vehicle.

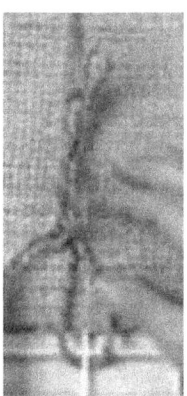

8. On the same side of the vehicle, lead the rope around another anchor point. Then, you can toss the rope over the load to the farther side. Repeat the above procedures starting from the second one.

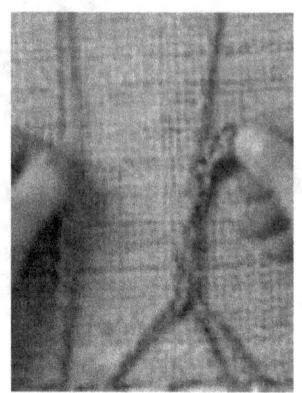

Ocean Plait

This knot is used as a table mat, doormat, a decorative insignia attached to uniforms, or for wall décor.

Procedures

> 1. Make an overhead loop in the counterclockwise direction with one end of a long rope.

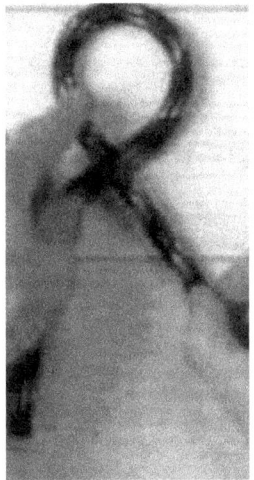

2. Turn the working end of the long rope around and then, lay it over the standing end of the initial loop.

3. Pick the end of the rope and lay it over the top loop.

4. Pass the working end in a diagonal direction and lay it across the lower loop.

5. Pick the other half of the rope, which is the running end. Then lay the working end over the new standing part of the rope.

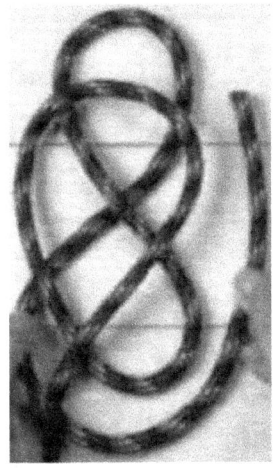

6. Tuck in the end of the rope diagonally through the loop nearest to it.

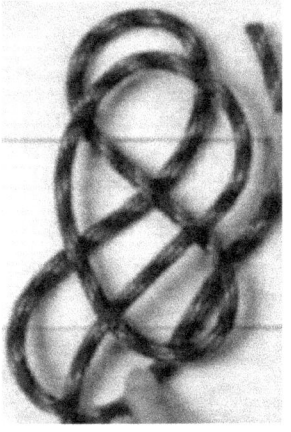

7. Pick up the running end and run it diagonally from right to left under the knotted parts of the rope.

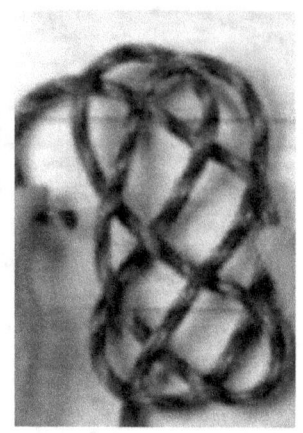

8. Tuck the running end of the rope diagonally while going over so that it comes at the bottom right.

9. Tuck the running end along with the standing part while following the original lead to double or triple the knot.

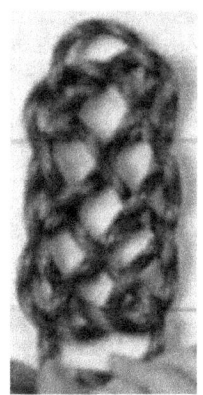

Hiking Knot

This is a knot you tie when you are going hiking (also called sheet bend). It is used for joining two ropes of different diameters.

Procedures

1. Bend the denser of the two ropes into the shape of a fish hook.

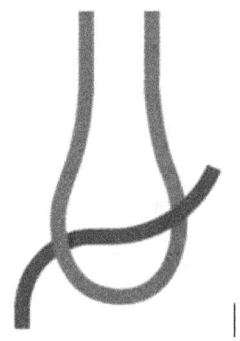

2. From the other side, pass the bent rope through the fish hook.

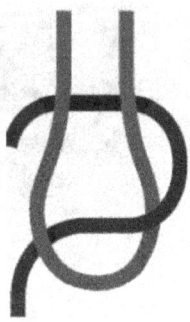

3. Wound the rope around the fish hook immediately.
4. Tuck the smaller rope under itself.

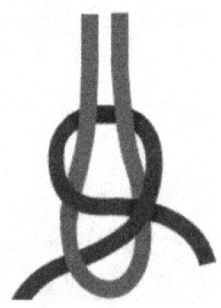

Square Knot

This type of knot is used in tying bondages, packages, shorter ropes together as well as in tying bundles of firewood.

Procedures

1. Lap the right of one end of a rope over the left of another end of a rope

2. In the opposite direction, tie continuously, i.e., left over right until you get a square knot as shown below

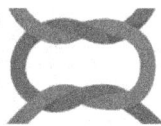

Two-Half Hitches

This type of knot is used in securing lines to tress, rock, or pole.

Procedures

1. Use the rope to wound around a tree, pole, or rock

2. Wound around the line twice and in the same direction, then pull tightly.

Sailor's Knot

This bend is known as carrick bend. It can be used to join ropes together. It is also easier to unknot this tie than it is to unknot a square knot.

Procedures

1. Make a simple loop with the bigger of the two ropes that you get. Set the loop on top of the running end of the second rope.

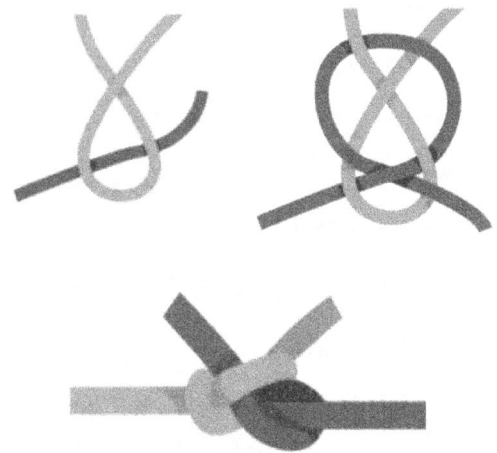

2. The pattern you follow for this project is this — over, under, over, under...

3. The ends will pop out of the opposite sides of the knot.
4. Leave the ends to the rope's standing part.

Fishing Knot

This knot is used to fasten a hook to a fishing line (also called palomar knot). With this, you can even attach a fly to a leader.

Procedures

1. Make a double length of a 6-inch line before you pass it through the eye of the fishing hook.

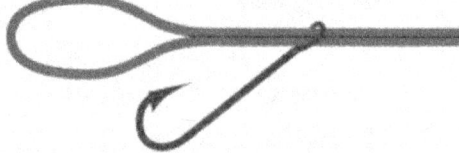

2. Tie an overhand knot that is not too tight with the hook hanging from the bottom.

3. Move the loop over the fishing hook. To do this, pass the loop above the hook's eye.
4. Tug on either end of the fishing hook and then tighten the knot onto the hook's eye. Clip the end of the knot.

Bowline Knot

This knot is used for camping. With it, you can form loops at the end of ropes that won't shrink or slip. This knot is used to secure traps and for climbing mountains.

Procedures

1. Form a small loop on one end of the rope.
2. Pass the free end of the rope through the loop while bringing it behind the line.
3. Take the free end down in the real loop while keeping the secondary loop. It is this secondary loop that ends up becoming the bowline loop.
4. Tug at the ends of the rope to tighten the knot.

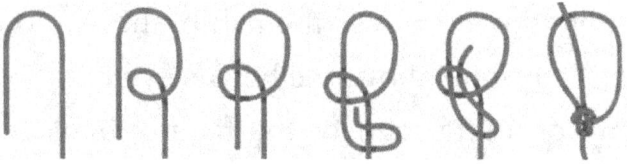

Eight-Strand Square Plait

This strand is used for scaling up fishing lines that you'd use to catch big sea mammals. It is also used to make leashes for dogs.

Procedures

1. Bring eight different strands together and then separate the strands into two groups—a left hand and a right hand, each of four strands. Start weaving the outermost strand around and behind the other strand so that it comes out in the middle of all the strands. This way, you can ensure that the outermost strands lie inside the other three strands back on its left side.
2. Like it was stated above, pass the outermost and right-hand strand behind the work o that it comes out to be in the middle of all the strands. This way, the outermost strand can come back to its right side.

3. Do step 1 again to be sure that the topmost strand is the one that is fixed to the farthest side.
4. Do step 2 again while ensuring that you choose the one farthest away.
5. As you go through each step, make sure you work to tighten the knot. As each strand moves to the back, increase the tension you apply on it. Then, when you are done, join the ends.

Three-Strand Braid

This knot is one of the commonest kinds of braid you'd find. It is used to make the tails of horses and long human hair.

Procedures

1. Bring the three strands together before separating them into a single strand that is quite displaced to the left. After, you'd make another pair of strands to the right.
2. Take the outermost thread that is fixed to the right to lie inside the strand to the left hand side.
3. Bring the outermost of the pair of strands at the left hand side across the front to lie inside and below the strand to the right.
4. Do step 2 again while pulling on the knot and tightening it as you move ahead.
5. Do the step 3 again while pulling the ropes with the same force as you continue.
6. Do step 2 again while making sure to take the last working strand into the pair at the farthest end.
7. Continue weaving the strands alternate to one another until you get the length you need. After, bind the ends so tightly that they don't loosen after.

Two-Strand Braid Knot

This knot is used to embellish land yards. You could try these projects with two ropes of the same color, but it is interesting to use different colors. You could even try using two different materials with different textures. Although, as you work, you might need to check the tension that you apply on each step's knot so that you do not come out with a final project that is too loose.

Procedures

1. Find the middle of two lengths of rope, and then interlock their bights together at those points.

2. Leave a distance equal to the length of the desired knot by separating the ends of the bights. After, you can separate the four ends of the rope into the left and the right parts.
3. Take the outermost strand, which is located towards the right hand strand towards the back and then, tuck it into the front of the weave from the back. Make sure you are moving in between the two strands by the left side.
4. Loosen the loose strands from the bight you formed and then take the outermost strand to the left side and then tuck it up from the back. Make sure the knot formed lies between the two strands and is located to the right side.
5. Do steps 3 and 4 again until the closed bight has some space for one final tuck.

Braid Knot

This knot can be used as a makeshift handle for a suitcase or for a dagger plate.

Procedures

1. Make a long underhand loop to the clockwise direction with the three cord parts parallel to each other.
2. Start the braid by moving the right hand strand over the middle strand so that it lies inside and below the left hand strand.
3. Pass the left hand strand over the middle strand to lie inside and under the right hand strand.

4. Do step 4 again, while taking care to note that the outermost strand becomes the running end each time.
5. Do step 3 again while ensuring that you follow the principle that strand you don't work much with becomes the next working strand.
6. Continue braiding alternate strands; the one to the right and the one to the left, while tugging the ends of the rope as you continue with each knot.
7. Untangle the rope's outer edges as you continue by regularly pulling out the project's single working end. This technique will help get rid of the mirror image that is formed during the final braiding process.
8. Tighten each knot as you continue while applying the right tension on it so that the final loop is pushed towards the end of the knot.
9. Lastly, tuck in the rope's working end through the rest of the loop to hold the braid in place.

Endless Double Chain

This kind of knot is used as a body ornament. Even though the pictures below show two different colors, the project is usually done with the aid of the two ends of a single cord.

Procedures

1. Get the standing and the working ends of the double chain close to each other.
2. Pass the running end from the back of the knot to the front while moving through the standing end's last loop.

3. Tuck the end up through the knot, i.e., besides itself, starting from the back to the front.
4. Tuck the working end from the front to the back, under one knot, through its loop.
5. Tuck the end to the side starting from the top to the bottom of the rope as the second loop is picked from the starting point again.
6. Lead the running end up from the back of the knot to the front while going under to cause it to leave from the third of the working end loops.
7. Lastly, tuck the end down from the front to the back by going under the knot to meet with the line's standing line.

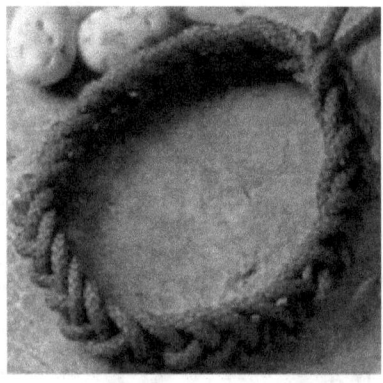

Endless Simple Chain

This knot can be joined to the ends of a simple chain, and during these times, the chain usually keeps its shape. You can use it to make bracelets, anklets, or to frame pictures. In the illustrations below, you'd see two ropes of different colors, but then, this project only employs the use of one cord.

Procedures

1. Take the beginning of the chain and its end. Then, bring them together.
2. Tuck the final end—here, it is the one to the left—through the starting loop from the back to the front by following the standing end.
3. Take the working end from the back to the front through its own loop by laying it beside its length.
4. Take the end of the chain to the right, from the front to the back, while passing through the loop adjacent to it. This loop in question is the one you made in step 3.
5. Take the rope's standing end away from the first tuck and then replace it with its working end.

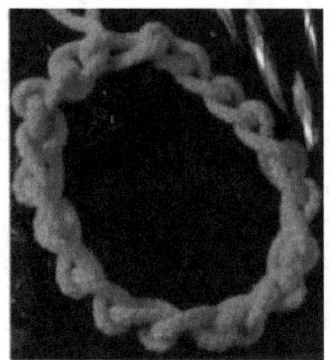

Clove Hitch

It is used to quickly secure a line to a post or tree, and also, used to fasten a shelter together.

Procedures

1. Make a loop of rope around the tree. Make another loop, passing the free end underneath the second loop, then tighten.

Taut Line Hitch

This knot is commonly used to anchor a tent

Procedures

1. Wound rope around a tree or post many feet away from the free end.
2. Working backward the post, the free end should be coiled twice around the standing line.

3. One coil around the standing line should be made on the outside of the coils you just made. Then tighten the knot, sliding it to adjust the tension.

Chapter 5

Resolving Knot Tying Common Mistakes

1. It is dangerous for you not to check your knots twice if you are using it for jumping purposes. You have to make sure that the rope is well threaded through the belay device and that the carabineers are well locked.
2. To make the perfect knots, you need more confidence than competence. For this, you have to take your time to make those right knots. Watch out for the kind of pressure you exert on each knot too.
3. Do not forget to knot the end of the rope you have just knotted. You could end up losing all your knots or even your life if you climb mountains with such unknotted ropes.
4. When trying to unknot a knot, do not hit it with a hammer too hard. This could lead to the fibers of the rope snapping open.

5. Note that the strength possessed by a knot is lost when the rope bends around an object. This loss of strength is because the rope's outer curve might have to support all the weight, which can lead to serious problems with straining.
6. Do not pass your rope over sharp edges, as they can cut through the rope until it finally snaps into two.

The end… almost!

Hey! We've made it to the final chapter of this book, and I hope you've enjoyed it so far.

If you have not done so yet, I would be incredibly thankful if you could take just a minute to leave a quick review on Amazon

Reviews are not easy to come by, and as an independent author with a little marketing budget, I rely on you, my readers, to leave a short review on Amazon.

Even if it is just a sentence or two!

So if you really enjoyed this book, please...

\>\> Click here to leave a brief review on Amazon.

I truly appreciate your effort to leave your review, as it truly makes a huge difference.

Chapter 6

Knot Tying Frequently Asked Questions

1. What are the preliminary knots I should take note of when scouting?

There is the square knot, the sheet bend, the clove hitch, the two half hitches, the taut-line hitch, the overhand knot, timber hitch, and the figure-eight knot.

2. How can I tie a rope to its length?

First, you have to form a loop that you can lay upon the rope you want to tie its other end to. Next, roll the rope into 3 parts, leaving them to be within the loop. Then, see that the three rolls you made earlier are next to each other. Then, you can tug hard at the ends of the knot to tighten it.

3. How do you loosen a tight knot?

There are several ways by which you can get this process done. You could hit the knot lightly with a hammer, submerge it in water, untwist one end of the knot and force it out through the loop, and so on.

4. What is the strongest knot I can tie?

The strongest knot is the Palomar knot. It is used for fishing and to make it, you will need to follow only three techniques or procedures. The toughness of this knot is attributed to the lack of twists and knots within it.

5. What is the strongest stopper knot I can tie?

The figure-eight stopper knot is the strongest knot. It is mostly employed in sailboats. The knot looks just like the figure eight.

6. What kind of knot gets tight when you tug at its ends?

The arbor knot gets tighter as you tug at the ends. This knot is based on the noose knot.   The arbor knot is also used to compress loads and weights such as sleeping bags.

7. Are splices stronger than knots?

Yes, splices are stronger than knots. They are more permanent too. The only issue with splices is that it takes a longer time to make them, unlike most knots.

Conclusion

Knot tying is one that is quite simple and easy to do, as long as you follow the necessary instructions and guidelines. All you need to get are ropes, either synthetic or natural, whilst taking time to see that your choice suits your needs. Apart from all the tips and techniques discussed in this book, you might have to work with some other tools like netting needles of various sizes, gripfids of small and big sizes, wire loops, jeweler's pliers, round-billed pliers, and so on.

As regards the projects listed in this outline, attack them with as much confidence as you can muster. If you want to be a professional in the art of rope-tying, you will need to try out the projects over and over again. You should not tug at the ends of the rope too tightly. You also shouldn't apply too little pressure. Abide by all the rules and safety guidelines outlined here, and you will be fine.

Happy knotting!

www.ingramcontent.com/pod-product-compliance
Lightning Source LLC
Chambersburg PA
CBHW050325120526
44592CB00014B/2060